MUSCLES TO MACHINES

Design	David West
	Children's Book Design
Editor	Margaret Fagan
Picture researcher	Cecilia Weston-Baker
Illustrator	Alex Pang
Consultant	Alan Morton PhD
	Science Museum, London

© Aladdin Books 1990

First published in the
United States in 1990 by
Gloucester Press
387 Park Avenue South
New York NY 10016

ISBN 0-531-17200-7

Library of Congress Catalog
Card Number 89-81596

Printed in Belgium

HANDS·ON·SCIENCE

MUSCLES TO MACHINES

NEIL ARDLEY

GLOUCESTER PRESS
New York · London · Toronto · Sydney

CONTENTS

This book is about movement — from the movement that humans make using their muscles, to the machines we use to travel at high speed or lift huge weights. The book tells you about the different ways that things can move, and it describes the forces that work to slow down movement, like friction. There are "hands on" projects for you to try which use everyday items as equipment. There are also quizzes for fun.

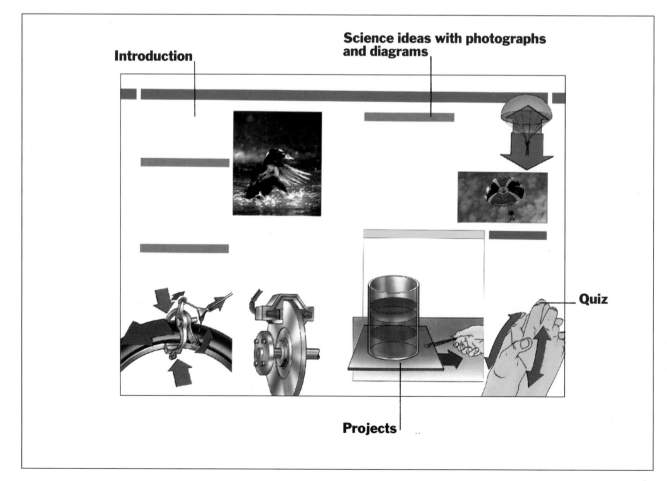

Introduction

Science ideas with photographs and diagrams

Quiz

Projects

Introduction

Nearly everything we do involves movement, from walking down the street to throwing a ball or lifting a heavy box. Human movements like these are made by using our muscles, which contract and relax to move our bones. In the very earliest times, nearly all work had to be done using the muscle power of human beings or animals like horses and oxen.

But if we want to travel faster than a horse can gallop, or lift something that is very heavy, we have to use machines. Even simple machines like levers and pulleys enabled ancient engineers to build pyramids and construct huge stone buildings. Today we have cars, trains and planes to carry us at high speeds. Construction engineers use tall tower cranes to build skyscraper office buildings. But all of these, from muscles to machines, involve movement.

A photograph of muscles that have been magnified.

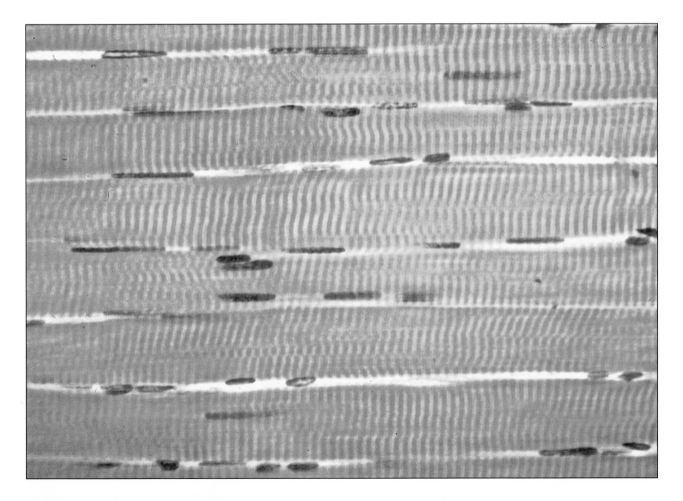

Things need a push or pull to get them moving. We call this push or pull a force. We exert a force whenever we use our muscles. We use small muscles in our face to blink an eye or smile, and large muscles in our legs to run and jump. Muscles and movement are involved in practically everything we do.

MUSCLE POWER

Muscles work by contracting, or getting shorter. Every muscle that produces movement is made up of bundles of thin fibers. And each fiber consists of bundles of even finer strands. When a muscle contracts, these strands slide past each other so that the muscle shortens.

When a muscle relaxes, the opposite action happens. The fine strands in the muscle fibers slide back to their original positions and the whole muscle lengthens. A muscle is usually "told" to contract or relax by messages sent along nerves from the brain. But some muscles, like those that control your heartbeat and breathing, work automatically. They do not need to be told when to act, and continue working all our lives.

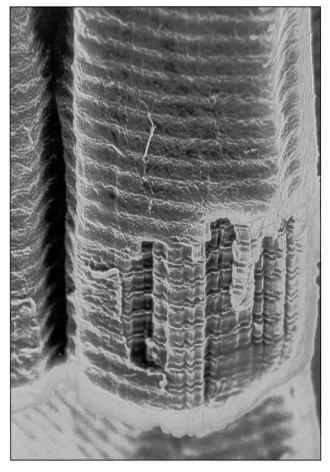

△ Muscles consist of many bundles of very fine fibers that slide past each other to make the muscle contract, or shorten.

MUSCLES AND MOVEMENT

Muscles are attached to bones by tough, fibrous tissues called tendons. The big muscle in the front of your upper arm, for example, is joined to your lower arm just below the front of your elbow. When you bend your arm, the elbow joint acts like the pivot of a lever. The upper arm muscle contracts, and pulls your forearm toward it. If you hold the inside of your elbow while bending your arm, you can feel the tendons working.

When you straighten your arm, a muscle in the back of your upper arm contracts. It pulls a tendon that passes over the point of your elbow. You can feel the tendon with your other hand.

△ Bowling makes use of most of your muscles — in the legs, back and arms. The ball is finally launched by the muscle-powered lever of the arm.

MOVEMENT AND FORCE

When you use muscle power to throw a ball, you use a force to cause movement. The ball continues to fly through the air after it leaves your hand. This is because once something has started to move, it does not need any force to keep moving. The ball moves at a certain speed, or velocity. If its speed is fast, it covers the distance to its target in a short time.

If a force continues to act while an object is moving, so that it gets more energy and accelerates, its speed increases. This happens when you start riding a bicycle. You pedal hard at first and the force of your leg muscles pushes the bicycle along the road.

△ Athletes starting a race use as much force as possible to get moving. The more force they exert, the faster they run.

MAKE A POPGUN

Use your muscles to exert enough force to power a gun. Take a soft plastic container, like an empty dishwashing soap bottle. Remove the top and push a cork into the container.

Now, press the sides of the container. The cork or paper will fly out at high speed and shoot across the room. Take care not to hit anyone or do any damage.

When you press the sides of the container, the air presses on the cork with a force that is strong enough to make the cork fly out.

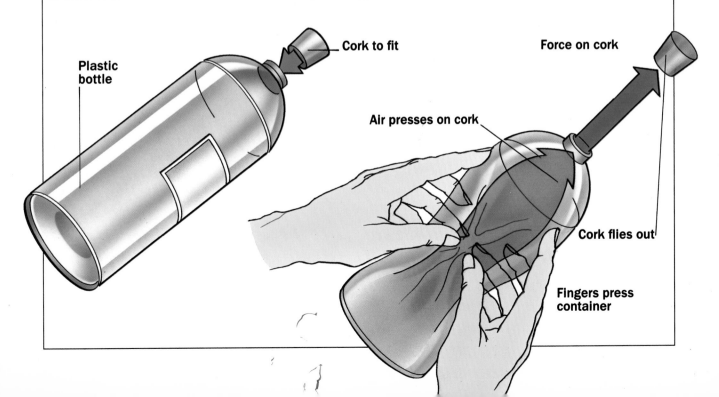

Cork to fit

Plastic bottle

Force on cork

Air presses on cork

Cork flies out

Fingers press container

All of us experience the force of gravity. It is a force that acts between an object and the Earth, and it makes things fall by pulling them down. Gravity also keeps everything resting on the ground or on the floor. Gravity still acts on everything, even though the ground or floor prevents movement. It gives everything weight.

FALLING

When you use your muscles to throw a ball up in the air, the force of gravity pulls down the whole time. It first acts in the opposite direction to the upward movement of the ball so that the ball's speed lessens. When the ball stops for a moment at the top of its climb, gravity still pulls on it and it begins to fall back down to Earth. The size of the force of gravity that pulls an object down is the same as its weight. The weight depends on its mass — the amount of matter in it. Gravity makes the speed of falling objects increase at the same rate, whatever their weight.

FLYING

Birds, aircraft and balloons are all able to overcome the force of gravity. They can float or fly. This is because they all produce a force called lift that pushes them upward. The lift is stronger than the force of gravity pulling them down. As a result, they move upward and rise.

The wings on birds and aircraft produce lift as they move through the air. The wings must move fast, which is why aircraft have to rush along a runway to take off. Birds use muscles to flap their wings to get enough lift and fly. Balloons get their lift from the hot air or gas they contain.

Once in flight, lift may lessen. When it becomes equal to gravity, the bird, aircraft or balloon stays at the same height. If lift lessens further, gravity will be greater and the object will descend.

△ Gravity makes things fall. The steeper the slide, the more effect gravity has, and the faster you slide down.

Fill one box with a material like sand

Force of gravity

Drop them from the same height exactly together

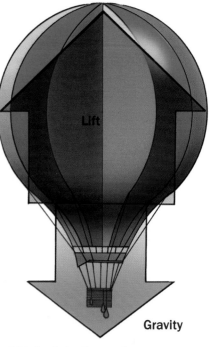

◁ Hot-air balloons have burners that heat the air in the balloon. The hot air is lighter than the cool air around the balloon, and produces lift.

FAST OR SLOW?

Drop two boxes, one of which is empty and one full. Guess which will hit the ground first. They always fall together whatever their weight.

Roll two balls made of plasticine down a slope. Let them go at the same time. Both balls move together because gravity pulls them down.

Make clay balls of different sizes

Part of the force of gravity

Board raised at one end

QUIZ

How much would you weigh on the Moon? In fact, you would have only a sixth of your weight on Earth. This is because the Moon is smaller than the Earth. Its force of gravity is only a sixth of the Earth's gravity.

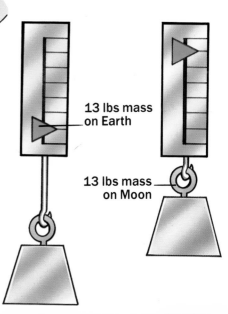

13 lbs mass on Earth

13 lbs mass on Moon

Forces always act between two objects; one object must push or pull on another. Forces also come in pairs that act on both objects in opposite directions. The jet engines on an aircraft produce a powerful force that pushes air backward. A force in the opposite direction pushes the engines — and the aircraft — forward.

▽ Action and reaction cause a cannon to recoil when it fires. As the cannonball shoots from the barrel, the cannon recoils or jerks backward. Two forces act: the action moves the cannonball, the reaction moves the cannon.

PAIRS OF FORCES

When you walk, muscles act in pairs to move your legs. As you step forward, your feet push backward on the ground. You can discover this for yourself if you step on some ice: your feet slip back and you may lose balance and fall over. But normally, your feet grip the ground. As you push against it, the ground exerts an equal force on your feet.

The force with which you move your feet is the action. The equal and opposite force with which the ground pushes back is the reaction.

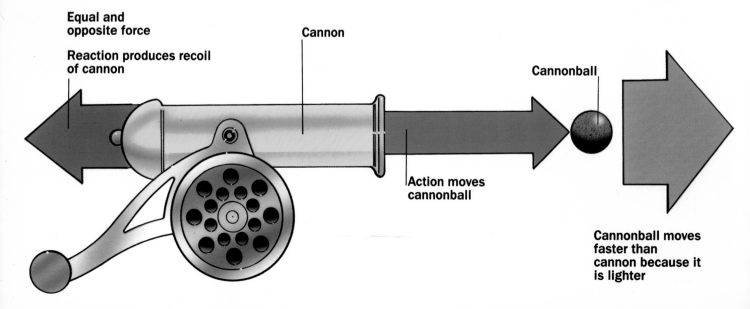

Equal and
opposite force

Reaction produces recoil
of cannon

Cannon

Cannonball

Action moves
cannonball

Cannonball moves
faster than
cannon because it
is lighter

FEELING THE FORCES

It is difficult to get an idea of action and reaction because you may not feel both of these forces when you move. When you walk, for example, you are not really aware of the ground pushing on you. But you can feel how action and reaction operate if you are able to move easily. Put on some roller skates and throw a large ball forward. As you throw the ball, you will move backward on the skates.

△ The action of the skater produces a reaction from the ice, which moves the skater forward.

Heavy ball

Action moves ball forward

Reaction moves skater backward

SEEING THE REACTION

Blow up two balloons and tie the necks. Fix a short straw to each one with sticky tape. Thread the balloons on a long piece of string. Untie the neck of the first balloon, and it will shoot along the string at high speed. The reaction to the force of the escaping air drives the balloon forward. The second balloon moves back as air escapes from the first.

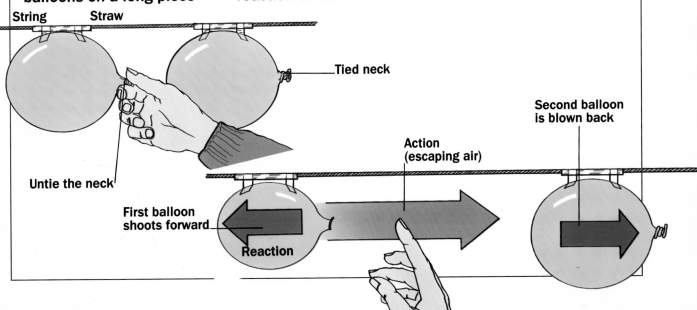

String   Straw

Tied neck

Second balloon is blown back

Untie the neck

First balloon shoots forward

Action (escaping air)

Reaction

Things seldom move in straight lines. They generally change direction as they move, turning to right or left, or rising or falling. They may also move faster or slower. This is because forces acting on them are constantly changing. A ball moves in a straight line unless acted upon by another force like the wind.

SLIDING AND SKATING

Moving at a steady speed in one direction does not require any force at all. Balls rolling over a flat surface move in this way. But most movement needs some force to continue; you need to pedal a bicycle, for example, to keep it moving.

Once something is moving, it will continue to move without force. People sliding on ice move in this way. They get up speed by running, and then slide over the ice without any further action. There's little force to stop sliders or to make them change direction. They move easily in a straight line at the same speed.

Sliding and skating on ice is great fun. You move effortlessly because the skate blades have a very smooth surface.

CHANGING DIRECTION

Once on the move, an object will change direction only if a force pushes or pulls it to one side. When the side force stops, the object continues moving in a straight line, but in a new direction.

Kicking a football to score a field goal can be very difficult. You can use enough force to reach the goal and aim straight for it, but the ball still misses the net. Other forces cause it to change direction. Gravity makes it fall while a wind can turn it.

Steering a vehicle causes a side force to act on it. Turning the rudder of a boat makes water push on the stern so that the boat heads on a new course. The front wheels of a bicycle or car steer in the same way.

△ A person on skis moves with great speed across the snow, using balance to change direction.

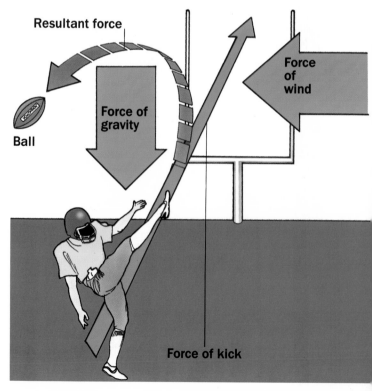

Resultant force

Force of wind

Force of gravity

Ball

Force of kick

FASTER AND FASTER

Riding a bicycle downhill is exciting. You do not need to pedal, yet you go faster and faster. The force of gravity pulls you down the slope, acting all the time to make you speed up.

This increase in speed is called acceleration. The force of gravity makes a falling object increase its speed by 33 feet a second for every second that it continues to fall.

The greater the force that acts on a moving object, the greater its acceleration. A powerful car has a big engine that produces a lot of force. It can therefore increase speed quickly and move ahead of other less powerful cars.

SLOWER AND SLOWER

After riding a bicycle down into a valley, you will be faced with getting up the other side. You now have to overcome the force of gravity, which pulls you back down the hill. Unless you start pedalling again, the bicycle loses speed and you go slower and slower. If you cannot pedal hard enough to overcome gravity, the opposing force will bring you to a stop.

A force acting in the opposite direction to the direction of movement causes speed to decrease. The loss of speed is called deceleration. It is sometimes necessary for a car to decelerate or stop rapidly. Powerful brakes produce a very strong force that slows the car quickly.

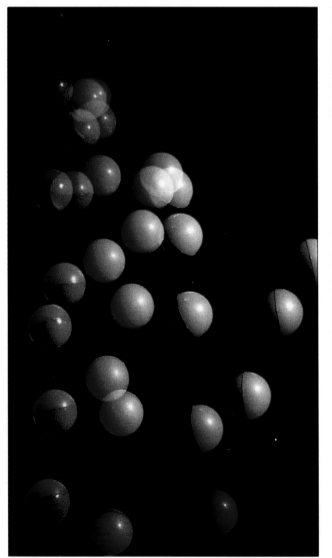

△ A bicyclist struggles to get up a hill. A lot of force is needed to overcome gravity and keep going.

◁ This ball was photographed several times as it dropped. It traveled farther between photographs because gravity made it accelerate.

Anything that is moving has kinetic energy. The bigger an object is and the faster it moves, the more energy it has. The kinetic energy of an object comes from the force producing movement, like muscles or motors. These sources have a supply of energy that they turn into kinetic energy.

BURNING FOR POWER

Cars, motorcycles, lorries, diesel trains and aircraft have internal combustion engines, which burn a fuel like gasoline, diesel fuel or kerasone. Burning produces heat, a form of energy, which the engine turns into kinetic energy. This kinetic energy then causes movement. Energy to move muscles comes from the "burning" of the food we eat.

ELECTRIC TRANSPORT

Electric trains have motors that use electricity to make things move. They do this by using the electric current to produce powerful magnetic fields that turn a shaft. Electric trains get their electricity from a cable or live rail. Diesel-electric trains have a diesel engine that drives an electric generator.

MOVEMENT OLD AND NEW

At first people used their own muscles or the muscles of animals like oxen to drive machines and vehicles. Muscles turn the energy in food into movement. An early machine to make movement was the waterwheel. This uses the energy of moving water to drive a shaft. Windmills work in the same way, but use the energy of moving air in the wind.

We still use these sources of movement today. Hydroelectric power stations contain turbines that work in the same basic way as waterwheels, and

△ A racing car develops a huge amount of kinetic energy. It contains a very powerful engine that burns gasoline.

▽ An electric train has a locomotive with a powerful electric motor, or several electric motors along the train.

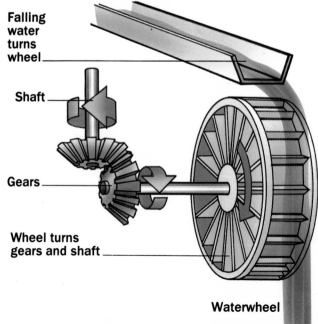

Falling water turns wheel

Shaft

Gears

Wheel turns gears and shaft

Waterwheel

wind generators are modern kinds of windmills. Both drive electric generators to produce electricity. These machines do not consume fuel to make electricity.

Wave generators turn the movement of waves in the sea into electricity. Solar cells turn the light of the Sun into electricity, which can then power an electric motor and produce movement.

▷ Windmills can be adapted so their sails drive generators to produce electricity.

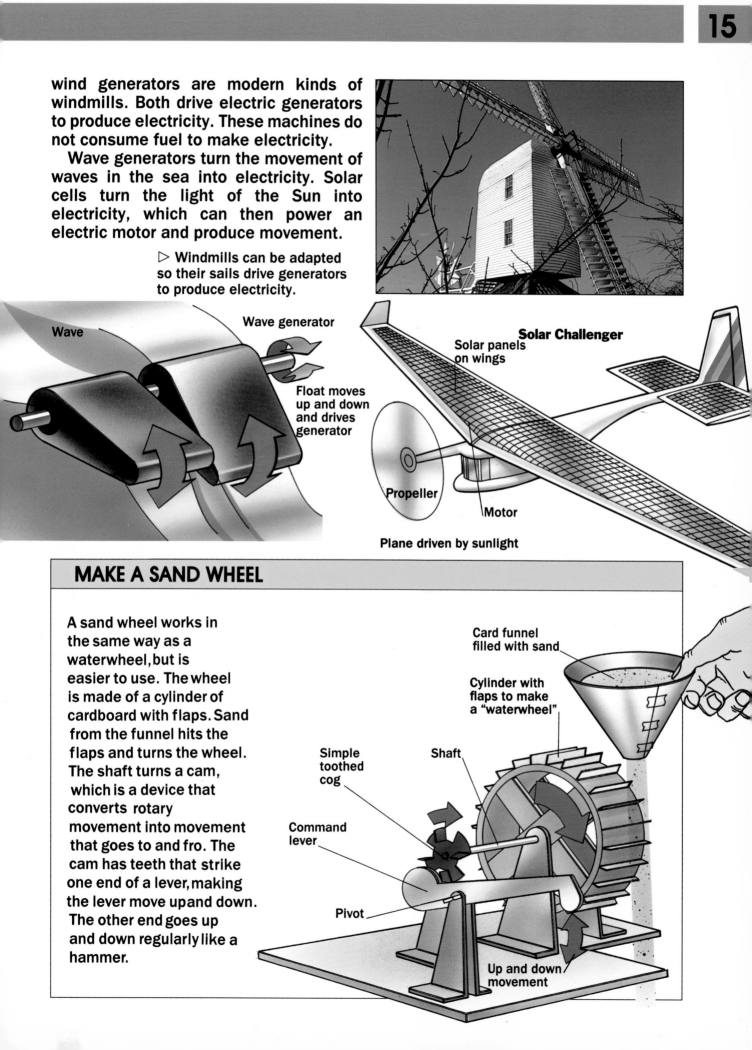

Wave

Wave generator

Float moves up and down and drives generator

Solar Challenger

Solar panels on wings

Propeller

Motor

Plane driven by sunlight

MAKE A SAND WHEEL

A sand wheel works in the same way as a waterwheel, but is easier to use. The wheel is made of a cylinder of cardboard with flaps. Sand from the funnel hits the flaps and turns the wheel. The shaft turns a cam, which is a device that converts rotary movement into movement that goes to and fro. The cam has teeth that strike one end of a lever, making the lever move up and down. The other end goes up and down regularly like a hammer.

Card funnel filled with sand

Cylinder with flaps to make a "waterwheel"

Simple toothed cog

Shaft

Command lever

Pivot

Up and down movement

It is easy to push a bicycle, but hard to push a car. We say that something has inertia if an effort is needed to get it moving. In fact, everything has inertia. A light object has a small amount of inertia, and a heavy object has a lot of inertia. The force required to stop something moving also depends on its inertia.

INERTIA IN ACTION

Getting a heavy car moving at a certain speed takes more energy and therefore more force than getting a light bicycle to move at the same speed.

Bicycles and cars have gears to help the engine or rider increase speed easily and therefore overcome the effects of inertia. Using a low gear when you start moving sends a lot of force to the wheels. The bicycle or car picks up speed quickly. Once something is moving, inertia resists any change in speed. Less force is needed and a higher gear can be used. Brakes exert a lot of force because inertia must again be overcome to slow and stop. Passengers have inertia too, and will jerk forward if they are free to move and the car stops suddenly. This is why you wear seat belts to prevent you from being pushed forward and injured when a car stops suddenly.

USING INERTIA

It is possible to make use of inertia when we need to keep something moving at the same speed. This happens in the turntable of a record player, which must turn at a constant speed. The turntable is heavy, and its high inertia prevents it from changing speed if the force of the motor driving the turntable alters slightly.

A flywheel is a heavy disk that is used in the same way in car engines. Some toys contain a flywheel connected to the wheels which keep them moving.

△ This tightrope walker is using a pole to balance. The inertia of the pole is small, and it can be moved quickly to help the walker balance.

▽ A shot putter can throw the shot only a short distance because it is heavy and has high inertia.

▷ Car engines make use of inertia. The up and down motion of the pistons is jerky. A crankshaft and flywheel attached to the pistons rotate and smooth out the motion. The constant motion then goes to the wheels.

Crankshaft rotates at constant speed

TOY TRUCK

Attach a string to a toy truck and fix a weight to the other end of the string. Place the truck on a table with the string over the edge. Let go: the weight pulls the truck quickly to the edge. Try again, but this time load the truck with some weights. Now the truck moves more slowly because the extra weight gives the truck more inertia.

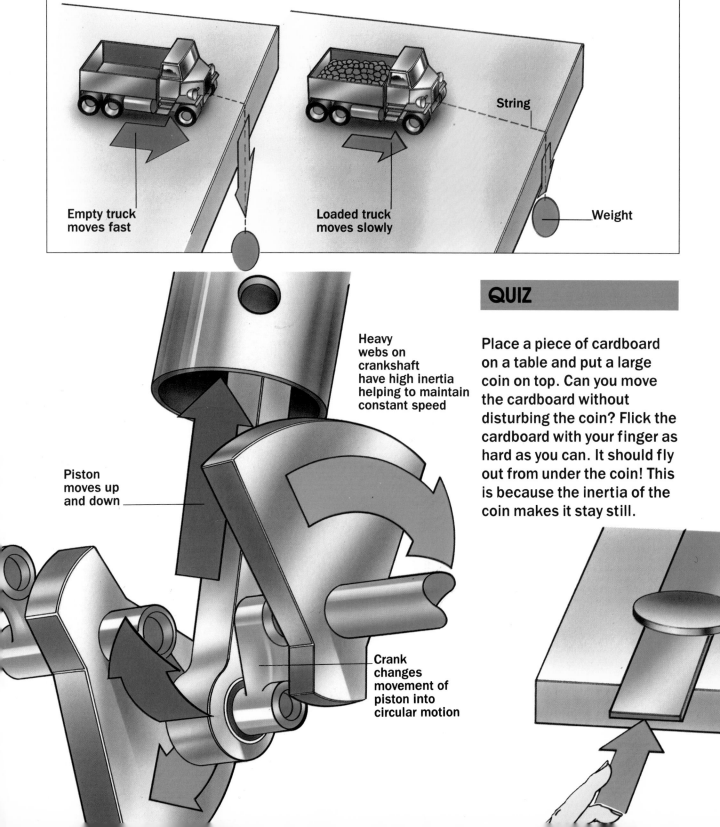

Empty truck moves fast

Loaded truck moves slowly

String

Weight

Heavy webs on crankshaft have high inertia helping to maintain constant speed

Piston moves up and down

Crank changes movement of piston into circular motion

QUIZ

Place a piece of cardboard on a table and put a large coin on top. Can you move the cardboard without disturbing the coin? Flick the cardboard with your finger as hard as you can. It should fly out from under the coin! This is because the inertia of the coin makes it stay still.

A moving object may collide, perhaps with another object on the move or with an obstacle. As it comes to a stop, the moving object loses its kinetic energy. This energy has to go somewhere; energy often goes to the other object which may start moving or change the energy it receives into heat.

TRANSFERRING MOTION

A moving object often collides with another that is free to move, like the balls in a game of pool or billiards. As one ball strikes another, it sets the other ball rolling. The first ball transfers kinetic energy to the second ball, which starts to move. It may transfer all its energy, so that the first ball comes to a stop. The second ball then moves off at the same speed as the first ball. If the first ball transfers only part of its energy, both balls continue to move at a slower speed.

△ Games like pool use collisions. The players use wooden poles to make one ball collide with another.

BOUNCING

A collision often results in a bounce. In this case, one or both of the objects is elastic, like a rubber ball. An elastic object changes shape when a force acts on it, but regains its shape when the force stops. The ball changes shape as it strikes the ground. Then it regains its shape, which causes it to push against the ground and bounce so that it also regains its kinetic energy.

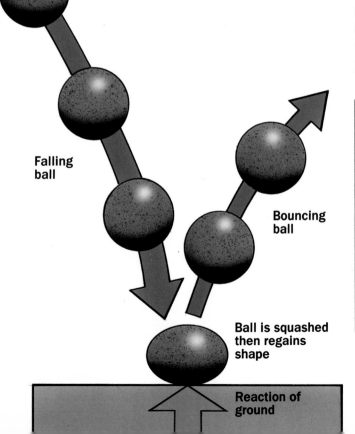

Falling ball

Bouncing ball

Ball is squashed then regains shape

Reaction of ground

△ Children can bounce on an inflatable because inflated objects are elastic.

ABSORBING MOTION

Not all collisions result in movement. Soft surfaces can absorb motion so that anything striking the surface stops. The objects in the collision absorb the kinetic energy of the moving object. The energy changes into sound (the noise of the collision) and into heat.

Springs are very good at absorbing energy. Sprung bumpers on a railway train can bring the train to a halt without damaging anything if a collision occurs at slow speed. Shock absorbers work in much the same way. In the human body, disks of cartilage between the bones of the spine act as shock absorbers when you land after a jump.

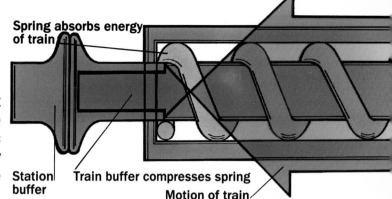

Spring absorbs energy of train
Station buffer
Train buffer compresses spring
Motion of train

▷ A train has bumpers to absorb movements between the carriages or trucks, which is important when the train stops.

COLLIDING COINS

Take some coins of different sizes. Tape two rulers to a table top so that they form a narrow channel. The coins should be able to slide easily along the channel.

Place a marker on one ruler a short distance along the channel. Put a coin by the marker, and flick another coin up the channel to strike the first coin. Note how far the coins move. Try different coins, and try to flick with the same force each time. See how lighter coins move farther. See also how flicking a heavier coin makes the other coin move farther.

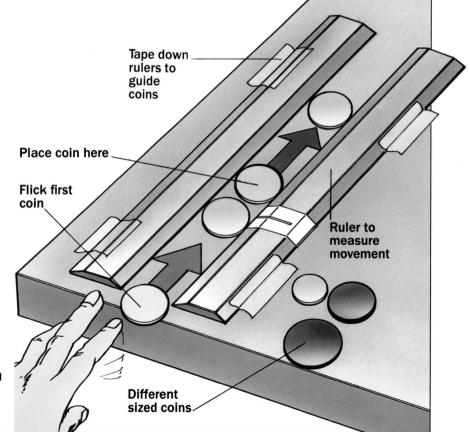

Tape down rulers to guide coins
Place coin here
Flick first coin
Ruler to measure movement
Different sized coins

All movements come to a stop unless force is used to keep things moving. The reason is that things rub against other surfaces, or even only against air or water, as they move. This contact produces friction, which slows and stops motion. In the human body, layers of cartilage reduce friction between bones.

FORCE AGAINST MOTION

As an object moves through air or water, it pushes the air or water aside. The air or water moves, taking some kinetic energy from the object, which moves slower. Sliding against another surface, especially if it presses hard, also takes energy and slows the object. In this case, the energy turns into sound and heat.

Friction is a force which always acts in the opposite direction to the movement. The size of the force varies, and falls to zero when the object stops.

△ A bird lands on some water, extending its feet to cause friction with the water and quickly bring it to a stop.

BRAKES

Friction is used to make brakes work. It provides an extremely strong force able to stop a fast moving car in several seconds. Bicycles have brake shoes that press against the rim of each wheel. Cars have disk brakes, in which pads press against a disk at the center of the wheel. Levers and pedals operate the brakes.

The pressure of the shoes on the rim or pads on the disk produces friction. Greater pressure gives a stronger force of friction and slows the bicycle or car more quickly.

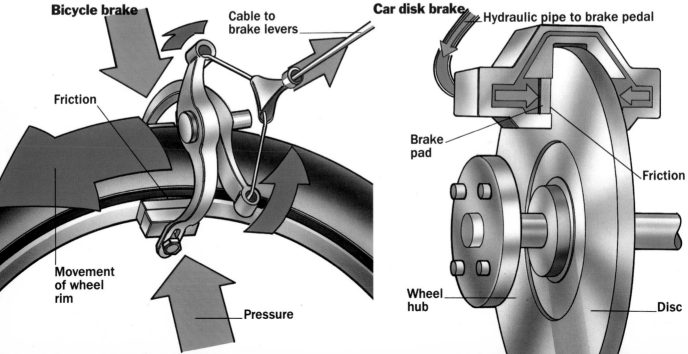

Bicycle brake

Cable to brake levers

Friction

Movement of wheel rim

Pressure

Car disk brake

Hydraulic pipe to brake pedal

Brake pad

Friction

Wheel hub

Disc

PARACHUTE

Parachutes make use of friction to lower people safely from the skies. People can use parachutes to escape from aircraft in emergencies, or if they make parachute jumps for sport.

When the parachute opens, it billows out and the large canopy pushes against the air. A strong force of friction develops between the parachute and the air. It acts upward to oppose the force of gravity pulling the parachutist down. The fall slows to a low speed at which the parachutist can safely land on the ground.

▷ Some parachutists like to fall freely through the air before opening their parachutes.

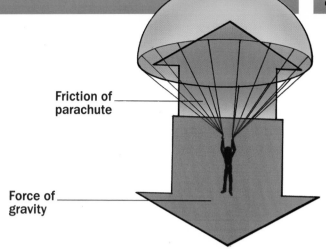

Friction of parachute

Force of gravity

DEMONSTRATE FRICTION

Put different amounts of water in the beaker

Fix a rubber band to a piece of cardboard. Place it on a table, and put a beaker of water on top. Pull the rubber band. It stretches before the cardboard moves. The amount of stretch shows the force of friction between the cardboard and the table.

Rubber band

Card

QUIZ

Why can you warm your hands by rubbing them together? Friction between the skin on your hands turns movement into heat. Press your hands very firmly together as you rub them. They get hotter because more friction develops and produces more heat.

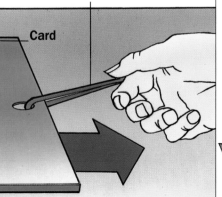

Friction is vital as a means of starting and stopping movement. But it is also a nuisance. Friction causes machines to waste some of the energy driving them by turning the energy to heat and noise. It lowers performance, and raises fuel consumption. We need ways of reducing friction to improve machines.

SLIPPERY SURFACES

You walk over the ground because your feet grip firmly. Friction between your feet and the ground stops them slipping and provides a good grip. Car tires are designed to grip the road strongly.

When a road gets wet, friction gets less. This happens because a film of water covers the road, and there is less contact with it. The tread on tires squeezes out the water film to maintain friction. A covering of ice greatly reduces friction, making the road very slippery and dangerous.

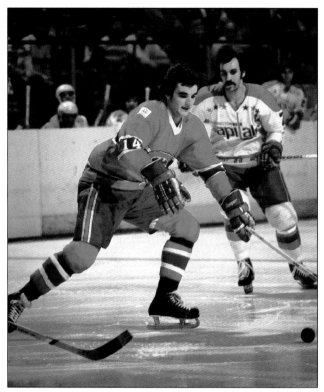

△ Skaters are freed from friction as they speed on ice. The surfaces of the ice and their skates are very smooth.

LUBRICATION

We can reduce friction in machines by lubrication. Oil is put into the machine, where it coats surfaces that rub and makes them slippery. All surfaces have tiny projections that catch against each other as they rub. Without lubrication, this would cause great friction, slowing and overheating the machine. The oil film separates the two surfaces so that their small rough spots do not catch.

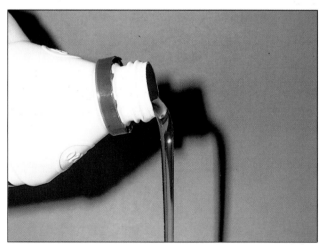

△ Oil lubricates the moving parts in the engine. Without oil, the engine would overheat and break down.

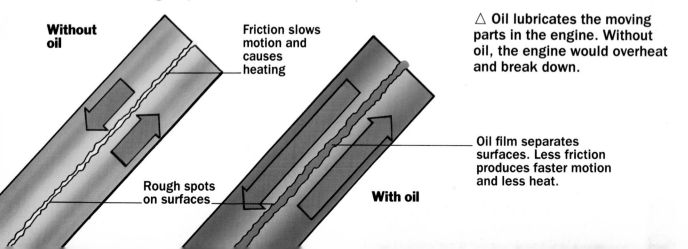

Without oil

Friction slows motion and causes heating

Rough spots on surfaces

With oil

Oil film separates surfaces. Less friction produces faster motion and less heat.

BEARINGS

Lubrication is not the only way to reduce friction in machines. Rolling is another way. Placing small steel balls or cylinders between two moving surfaces allows one surface to roll over the other just as a vehicle rolls over the ground on wheels. The balls or cylinders do not rub against the surfaces as they roll, so very little friction occurs.

A ball bearing contains a set of balls between two rings. The inner ring can rotate easily while the outer ring does not move. The bearing can be used to support a rotating shaft, which is fixed to the inner ring of the bearing.

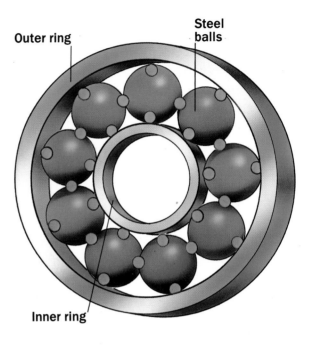

Outer ring
Steel balls
Inner ring

STREAMLINING

A third way of reducing friction is very important in transport, especially in aircraft. Streamlining gives the transport a shape that moves more easily through air or water. It has a pointed nose or bow and smooth sides, which do not push strongly against the air or water.

Reducing friction by streamlining an aircraft or car can give it a higher speed. Streamlining can also save fuel if speed is not increased.

▽ Many birds are streamlined so that they can swim at speed, catch prey and dive through the air or water.

TEST FOR FRICTION

Take two pieces of wood and put one on the other. Lay a hand on the top piece and try to move it. Friction is probably too strong. Now try placing safe liquids like soap between the two pieces and see how good they are for lubrication by reducing friction.

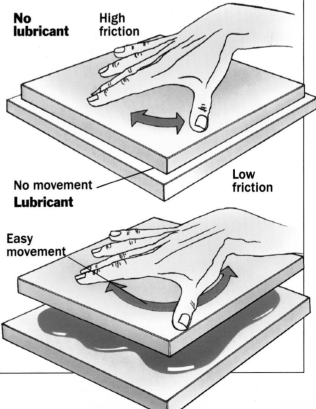

No lubricant High friction

No movement
Lubricant

Easy movement

Low friction

Things have energy when they are stationary as well as kinetic energy when they move. This stationary form of energy is called potential energy. It is "stored energy" that can be turned into kinetic energy to cause motion. When movement stops, kinetic energy may turn back into potential energy.

THE PENDULUM

Kinetic energy constantly changes to potential energy and back again in a pendulum. At the bottom of each swing, the weight moves fastest and has the greatest kinetic energy. Then as it rises, the pendulum begins to slow until it stops. The kinetic energy of the pendulum changes to potential energy, which depends on the height of the weight. As the weight stops, it has no kinetic energy, only potential energy. When it moves down again, its potential energy changes back into kinetic energy.

△ A trapeze artist swings to and fro to gain speed before soaring up into the air to grasp another trapeze.

Top of swing — greatest potential energy, no kinetic energy

Bottom of swing — greatest kinetic energy, no potential energy

Gains kinetic energy

Weight

Falling — potential energy changes to kinetic energy

Rising — kinetic changes to potential energy

STRINGS AND SPRINGS

Another form of potential energy depends on the length of an elastic string or spring. Changing the length takes energy, which the string or spring "stores" as potential energy.

A bow makes use of this potential energy. Pulling back the string stores potential energy in the string and bow as it stretches. When the string is released, its potential energy changes to kinetic energy as it fires the arrow.

Stretching or compressing a spring also stores potential energy. The spring moves back to its former length when it is released, changing its potential energy into kinetic energy. The spring in a toy or watch works in this way. Winding it up stretches a spring, which then drives the wheels of the toy or hands of the watch as it slowly regains its shape.

Bow stores potential energy

Bow releases its stored energy

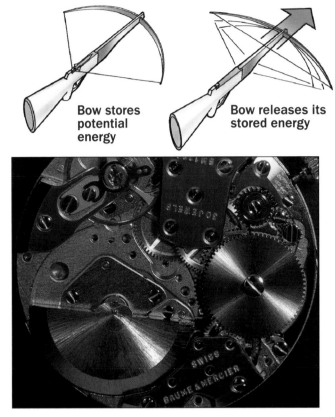

△ This clock mechanism contains a set of wheels driven by a mainspring to turn the hands.

▽ A roller coaster gives a thrilling ride as it swoops up and down. It is powered solely by the force of gravity.

FAIRGROUND RIDES

Many of the most exciting rides in fairgrounds or theme parks make use of potential and kinetic energy. You enter a car that is first hauled up to the top of a steep incline. Then the car plunges down a steep slope to begin a thrilling ride that takes you up and down more slopes and perhaps even around a circular loop.

The car speeds through all these ups and downs without a motor to drive it along the track. This is because the top of the incline is higher than any other part of the ride. The car gets a great store of potential energy, which then changes into kinetic energy as gravity pulls the car and it moves. This store of potential energy is enough to send the car through the complete ride, even up and around any loops in it.

Movement often happens in a circle or part of a circle. To turn a corner, you have to move around a section of a circle, for example. Circular motion is different from movement in a straight line. An object moves in a straight line without any force, but force is needed to keep something moving in a circle.

CENTRIFUGAL FORCE

As you zoom around on a fairground ride, you are pushed down in your seat. A strong force pushes you away from the center of the circle in which you are moving. This is called centrifugal force, but it does not really exist! What is happening is that the car is pushing against you as you move around in a circle.

Throwing the hammer, which is in fact a weight on a cord, shows the forces in circular motion. The thrower moves the hammer in a circle, and the weight flies out. In fact, the weight is trying to move in a straight line, but the cord pulls it into a circle. The thrower has to pull on the cord with a force called centripetal force to stop the weight flying away. When the thrower lets go, the weight carries on moving in a straight line.

△ A hammer thrower has to pull very hard and rotate as fast as possible before letting go of the hammer.

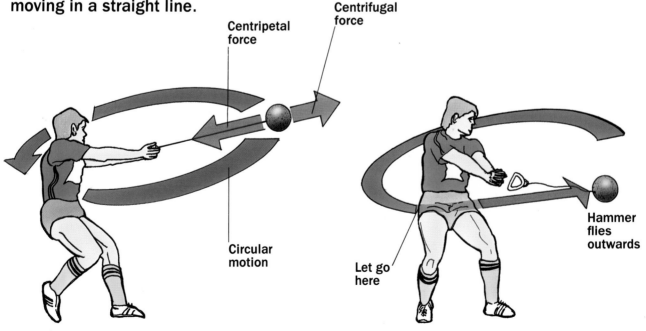

Centripetal force

Centrifugal force

Circular motion

Let go here

Hammer flies outwards

SPEED WITHOUT EFFORT

Try spinning on a revolving chair. If you tuck your legs in, you suddenly speed up. Now stick your legs out. You slow down. This effect happens because of the energy in circular motion. An object has more energy of movement when it is moving faster. Also, a wide object that is rotating has more energy than a narrow object of the same mass. When you pull your legs in, you suddenly become narrower. However, your total amount of energy does not change. Therefore, you move faster to keep the same amount of energy. Sticking your legs out makes you suddenly wider. To keep the same energy, you slow down.

△ A top can twirl on a point on the surface and spin faster and faster as you apply more force.

UPSIDE-DOWN WATER

Put some water in a bucket, grasp the handle firmly, pick it up and whirl it quickly around. At the right speed, the water will stay in the bucket, even if the bucket tilts upside-down. But get the speed wrong and the

Swing the bucket around

The water stays as if a force pushes it into the bucket.

water will slosh out, so take care. The water keeps trying to move straight on. You stop it by pulling the bucket in a circle. The water cannot flow toward the top of the bucket and stays inside.

QUIZ

Bicyclists and motorcyclists lean over when they turn a corner at speed. Why do they not fall over? Leaning over causes the centripetal force that pulls the bicycle or motorcycle into a circle. It enables the rider to make a sharper turn. Without leaning, the rider would fall outward.

Wheels rotate to move bicycles, trains and cars. We also use other wheels to produce motion. These are toothed wheels or gear wheels, which can change the speed at which the pedals power a bicycle or the engine drives a car. Gyroscopes are also rotating wheels and they move in an unusual way.

THE WHEEL AND AXLE

A wheel has an axle, a central shaft that turns to make the wheel rotate. The rim of the wheel moves faster than the axle. This enables you to speed along the road on a bicycle. The pedals pull the chain, which turns the axle of the back wheel. The rim of the wheel moves faster than the chain, so that the bicycle moves faster than your feet turn the pedals.

The chain passes over toothed wheels on the pedals and the back wheel. These two wheels are different sizes. If the hub wheel has half the number of teeth as the pedal wheel, it makes a full turn when the pedal wheel makes a half turn. Many bicycles have a set of hub wheels of different sizes that give different speeds. These are called gears.

BALANCING ON A BICYCLE

If you roll a coin along the ground, it will stay upright and move some way before toppling over. You are able to ride a bicycle because the rotating wheels, like the rolling coin, do not easily topple over. If you begin to tilt to one side while riding a bicycle, you move the handlebars slightly to swivel the wheel in the direction of the tilt. A strong force then moves the wheel back upright, and you keep your balance on the bicycle. This balancing movement is called precession.

△ The pedals turn the front wheel in a penny-farthing, an early form of bicycle.

16 teeth

16 teeth

Chain
Both wheels make one full turn

16 teeth

8 teeth

One full turn

One half turn

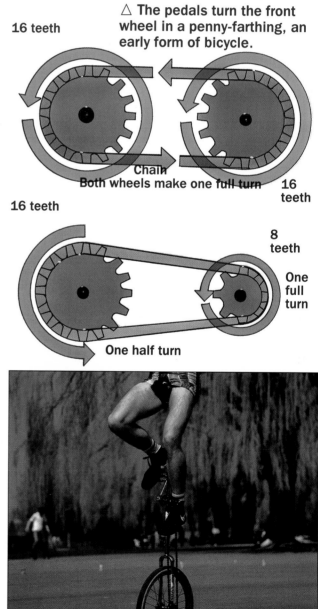

▷ Some riders can balance so well, that they can ride a unicycle.

GYROSCOPES

The gyroscope is capable of amazing feats of balance. A toy gyroscope can be made to stand on its pivot without falling over. The wheel in the gyroscope must spin very quickly to make it stand on its end. The gyroscope then begins to tilt and starts moving in a circle. After a while, the wheel slows and falls over. If it could be kept rotating, the gyroscope would continue to balance.

Precession occurs in the gyroscope. As it begins to tilt, the force of gravity pulls it down vertically. Another force acts to move the wheel in a horizontal direction, causing the whole gyroscope to move in a circle around the pivot. Gyroscopes can be used in very accurate compasses.

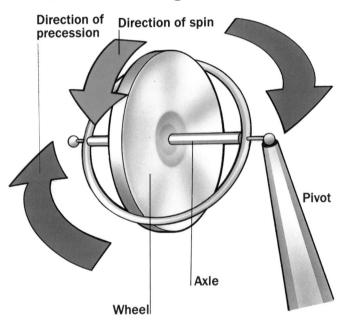

Direction of precession

Direction of spin

Pivot

Axle

Wheel

▽ Gyroscopes like this one make attractive toys but they can also be used in accurate instruments like a compass.

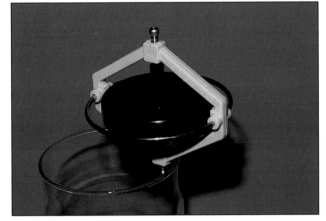

DEMONSTRATE PRECESSION

Remove the front wheel of a bicycle from its forks. Hold it upright by the axle and tilt the wheel slightly. Now ask someone to start the wheel spinning in the same direction as it would spin if you were riding the bicycle. Swivel the axle slightly. The wheel will move in an odd way and then right itself. This movement is called precession. It acts at right angles to the direction of the swivel. The movement keeps a bicycle upright when you pedal.

Precession rights wheel

Swivel the axle

Spin of wheel

It was not until about 400 years ago that scientists began to understand the forces that make muscles and machines move. Later, inventors were able to build engines for transport and, during the last hundred years, trains, cars and planes have become common. Here are some of the pioneering discoveries.

Galileo

Moving worlds

The famous Italian scientist Galileo (1564-1642) studied the way in which objects fall. He is said to have dropped two stones from the Leaning Tower of Pisa to show that they both reach the ground together. Galileo also believed that the Earth and other planets move around the Sun. The German scientist Johannes Kepler (1571-1630) studied the planets and worked out that they move in huge ovals around the Sun. However, he and Galileo could describe the forces acting on the planets.

Kepler

Newton

Gravity and the laws of motion

Isaac Newton (1642-1727), the British scientist, was able to describe how the force of gravity makes objects fall. He was led to this discovery by seeing an apple fall from a tree, and wondered whether gravity might also extend into space. He showed that gravity keeps the planets into their oval paths around the Sun. Newton described three laws of motion. The laws show that force does not sustain motion but only changes it; show how inertia affects motion; and show that action and reaction exist.

Daimler

The gasoline and diesel engines

Cars and aircraft need a powerful but light engine. The German engineer Gottlieb Daimler (1834-1900) made an important advance with the invention of the gasoline engine in 1885. Another advance came soon after with the invention of the simpler diesel engine in 1892 by Rudolf Diesel (1858-1913).

Acceleration
An increase of speed produced when a force continues to push or pull on an object. Acceleration is measured in meters per second per second.

Action
A force that is applied to produce motion.

Diesel engine
An engine, similar to a gasoline engine, in which the fuel burns without the need for a spark to ignite it.

Elastic
Able to stretch or bend and then regain shape. Substances like rubber are elastic, but so are materials like steel, which is often used to make springs or coils.

Energy
There are several forms of energy, including heat, light, sound, electricity, kinetic energy and potential energy. Energy is measured in joules.

Force
A push or pull that is applied to an object. If the object is not held, the force causes it to start moving. Force changes the motion of moving objects by changing their speed and direction. Force is measured in Newtons.

Friction
A force that occurs when two surfaces rub against each other, or when an object moves in a liquid or gas. Friction always acts to slow movement, and brings motion to a stop if no other force is applied to overcome it.

Gasoline engine
An engine that uses gasoline as a fuel. A spark causes it to burn in a cylinder and produce hot gases that move a piston. The movement of the piston then drives a shaft.

Gravity
A force that exists between any two objects and which acts to pull them together. The force of gravity is usually large enough to be noticed only when one or both of the objects is very massive, such as the Earth.

Inertia
A resistance to any change in movement that is possessed by everything. Inertia resists starting, stopping, speeding up, slowing down, and any change in direction. It has to be overcome in all these cases.

Kinetic energy
The energy of movement. Everything that moves has kinetic energy because it is moving and when it is moving. The amount of kinetic energy depends on the amount of matter and speed of the moving object.

Lift
A force that acts to lift an object, like an aircraft or bird, up into the air.

Muscle
A body tissue made up of bundles of fibers that can shorten to make the muscle contract. Muscles are needed for all bodily movements.

Potential energy
A form of energy possessed by everything that depends on its position or shape. An object gains potential energy if it is raised, for example.

Precession
A movement that occurs when a wheel rotates and its axle is made to swivel. The movement occurs at right-angles to the direction of the swivel.

Photographic Credits:
Cover and page 22: Allsport; pages 5, 6 top and 13 left: Science Photo Library; pages 6 bottom, 8, 11, 12, 13 right, 16 bottom, 20, 21, 23 and 24: Zefa; pages 7 and 27 top: Roger Vlitos; pages 9, 18 top, 25 top and 25 bottom: Spectrum Colour Library; pages 10, 14 bottom, 27 bottom, 28 top and 28 bottom: Robert Harding Library; pages 12 top, 16 top, 19 and 26: J. Allan Cash Library; page 15: Hutchison Library; page 18 bottom: Chapel Studios; page 29: Vanessa Bailey; pages 30 top, middle left and bottom: Popperfoto; page 30 middle right: Mary Evans Library.